The wolf's last verses © 2

All rights reserved.

No part of this publication may be reproduced, stored in a retrieval system, or transmitted, in any form or by any means, electronic, mechanical, photocopying, recording or otherwise, without the prior written permission of the presenters.

Amandine RZ asserts the moral right to be identified as author of this work.

Presentation by *BookLeaf Publishing*

Web: www.bookleafpub.com

E-mail: info@bookleafpub.com

ISBN: 9789360945695

First edition 2024

The wolf's last verses

Amandine RZ

BookLeaf Publishing
India | USA | UK

My goolf...

The shelf

I was there, sitting on a shelf
Dusty, opaque, rough diamond
Waiting for life to go by
I had no excitement, just

Watching people walk by
Watching relationships be undone
Watching life unfold
Watching me, alone

She walked by and said "oh hello"
Even dusty, opaque, she saw through me
Taking me from the shelf
She started to clean me up

I was putty in her hands
It felt so warm, so natural
I gave into the temptation
To fall into her oblivion

She tamed me, she liked to say
There was not one day
Where I did not think of her
As my forever partner

She broke me, she liked to say
I was fierce and independent
In my armor she made many dents
Feeling so cold when she walked away

Gardener

She painted flowers and rainbows
On the walls surrounding my heart
There were there for so long
Like an old companion

I did not see anything at first
Even when she asked for my number
We started chatting, bordering on harassing
But her messages were warming

In the depth of my heart and soul
She was indeed so beautiful
Before her, my life was black and white
Her patience was infinite

Piece by piece, she chipped away
At the door surrounding my garden
I did not want to shy away
I invited her to my den

In my garden she removed the weeds
Patiently waiting, tending to it
Watering everywhere she could
My garden was in full bloom

She gave me butterflies and flutterflies
She gave me the moon and the stars
I lost myself in her clear eyes
She was life's best surprise

I love her

I love her when she flashes her wonky smile
I love her stronger than the Nile
I love her when she laughs
I love her when she cries

I love her deeper than the oceans
I love her steadier than granite
I love her, she has so many qualities
I love her, she has so many flaws

I love her stronger than the diamonds
I love her with passion
I love her when she sleeps
I love her when she dreams

I love her when it rains
I love her when it's hot
I love her with all her quirks
I love her so, so much

I love her vastly
I love her deeply
I love her strongly
I love her lasting

I love her in summer, I love her in winter
I love her to the moon and back
I love her more than all the stars
I love her forever, for she is my sun

It does not even compare

I look at the stars in the sky
And realize they don't even compare
To the twinkle in her eyes
When in my eyes, she stares

I look at the moon in the dark
And realize it doesn't even compare
To the light she brings into my life
To the joy I feel in my heart

I look at the sun during the day
And realize it doesn't even compare
To the warmth she brought me
To the elation I feel in my body

I look at the waves in the ocean
And realize it doesn't even compare
To the force of the pull
I feel towards her, within my soul

I feel the wind on my face
And realize it doesn't even compare
To the healing powers of her smile
I wish she walked down the aisle

I feel the warmth of the fire
And realize it doesn't even compare
To the brasier she lit in me
I wish I still held her close to me

The change

She sees only the negative
She has not been lately so attentive
She listens to the noise in her head, caution
She does not care for my devotion

Did someone fill up her head
Did she lose her way somewhere
Did she not see my light
Coming to her through the night

I wish she would walk back on our path
But she gets deeper in the forest
Putting our love to the utmost test
In her head, feeling so much wrath

I don't know how to help
Except shine bright through the night
I don't know, she does not listen
Is she lost in her decision, so brazen?

I need her in my life
But I cannot force her to love me
This pain, in my heart, like a knife
She is the one for me

Wounded partners

I held her up when she couldn't stand
I fought for her when she had no strength
It was the right thing to do
I want to do right by her

Standing by her side
Looking at the ebb and flow of the tide
Taking her hand in mine
Wishing everything was fine

I thought I was doing good
I thought she'd guide me
I thought we had the deepest bond
I could not have been more wrong

I don't know what blinded me
I don't know when she stopped talking to me
She lost a friend so dear, how did I not see
The hurt, the pain, the dark shadow near

Lurking in her mind again
Maybe distorting reality, even
Thinking I walked in darkness
Telling me she had no more happiness

I could not believe it
I never thought she'd be that blinded
I never thought she'd give up on us
I feel betrayed like never

Rejection

She refused the ring I offered her
She smiled, she cried, I was in a tether
I will never give up on her
But she cannot see us together

I don't know what to do
To make us survive through
I only want to love her
Make her happy and be with her

I hope she gives me another chance
I hope she gives me another dance
To fall onto her lips
To realize she loves us heaps

I want to hold her
Forever and ever
I want to breather her in
Nights, days and in between

I am so in love with her
And it took me by surprise
But I got her, my babe,
We called it crazy love

The runaway heartbeat

The thumping of the heartbeat
Pumping blood, thumping in my ears
Racing forward, fleeing, wild
I cannot escape myself

I can run but I cannot run away
Heavy is my heart, heavy is the price to pay
I chose my mate for life
My mate rejected me

My mind is spinning around
What have I done, what does it mean
My heart is broken, my soul is crushed
What do I have to live for

Endless is my suffering
Just take the pain away
What a heavy price to pay
Feeling warm, freezing, led astray

Icy are the hands around my heart
Crushed are my hopes and dreams
Alone I will be
For it did not destroy me

I am alone

At night, being cold, alone
Missing my half, my love
Emptying my mind
To no avail, it's spinning around

Not knowing what to do or where to go
Cannot follow my gut, it's hollow
No will to go forward, to survive
Feeling the need to be revived

An empty shell of a wolf
A disgraced lady, misunderstood
Waiting for a sign, a ray of light
There are so many clouds

I cannot see through
I cannot breathe through
I cannot push through
I cannot think through

Survival instinct kicks in
Find refuge, time to lick my wounds
Cannot see a way out
Cannot see healing

So deep is the wound
So deep is the betrayal
So deep is the sorrow
Deep to my marrow

The oozing wound

How do I heal such a wound?
How do I keep going forward?
Where will my paws lead me?
Where will my mind take me?

An endless life of suffering
Not able to stop spinning
Wondering what I did wrong
Wondering why she did not fight

Mating was supposed to be
Vast, deep, strong and lasting
Gone is all hope and dreams
Gone is the will to live

Gloomy is my fate
Endless is my love
How can this all end
I am loyal to the death

Not able to love again
Not able to feel again
Or maybe I feel too much
My heart cannot take it anymore

So stabbing is my pain
So raw is my skin
So wet is my face
So bland is everything

My inner wolf

There moves a shadow
Wanting to get away from the meadow
Into the dark forest my wolf goes
Place of solace, silence and awe

The wind whispers in the trees
Words only my wolf can hear
For my wolf never sees
Betrayal come from within

Intense is the pain, takes the breath away
Yet my wolf wants to stay
Feel the pain, my wolf is alive
It takes more strength than I have

Staying immobile, a dark omen
Gave my heart but cannot come back to the den
What to do but run away
In the dark night like a stowaway

But my wolf is a fighter
Seems it led to my demise
For there is no honor
In breaking a promise

The hope to one day
Be reunited with my mate
The hope that the night will end
The hope to be whole again

Dying of love

Have you heard the bone chilling scream
Tree splitting, fog piercing,
Heart wrenching, soul destroying
Sound of the wolf dying of love

The forest goes silent
The water stops flowing
Everything stands still
A quiet homage

The lady of the forest
The shadow in the night
The silent runner
The faithful one

The tree branches are bowing
The leaves are shivering
Darkness hides the tears
The air stops existing

The birds stop chirping
The insects stop crawling
Dew covers everything
Silent goodbye in the forest shroud

The chills

Dark and cold is this night,
I try to fight it with all my might
But the darkness takes hold of me
Where am I, who am I, let me be

A cacophony of noises, such a mayhem
Somehow losing myself in them
The only time my mind stills
My body paralyzed, I have the chills

How I long for respite
My heart is heavy, like granite
Such an effort to draw a breath,
Could this be death?

Longing for the exquisite release
It won't come with ease
The shadows are beautiful
I feel so light, it's wonderful

Is that what it feels like?

Is that what it feels like
To walk in darkness when it's light
Keeping up a façade, keeping up a charade
Saying I'm ok when I die inside?

Is that what it feels like
To lose my most precious thing
To be amputated of my best part
To feel empty, to feel dark?

Is that what it feels like
To lose all hope in life
To stop smiling to others
To stop living, altogether?

Is that what it feels like
To be rejected by the one I trusted
To be betrayed, lied to
To question everything?

Is that what it feels like
To pretend, lie to myself
To take a step forward
To try to appear ok?

Is that what it feels like
To give more than I can
To never recharge, run on empty
To give up hope, be happy?

I miss her

Staring into the abyss
I miss her, I miss her so much
Her warmth, Her laugh
Her eyes, her smile

Her goodness, her golden heart
Her tenderness, her love
Her care, her amazingness
Her all, her weirdness

Such simple things in life
I miss without knowing
Fluttering in my stomach
Thinking of her, always

She is the one for me
The puzzle I love to solve
The rainbow woman covered in gold
The hope I didn't know I needed

She is the one for me
The light in the dark guiding me
The harbor that shelters me
The woman who completes me

They say it gets better with time

They say it gets better with time
They say we're going to be OK
They don't know how our hearts rhyme
They don't know our complicité

They really have no clue
How much I do love you
They don't know time stands still
Lost in each other's eyes, fulfilled

They just see another story
I know it's one for the ages
They say goodbye dearie
I know they don't see the damages

They think they know everything
I know they are not with us
Are they interfering?
I just want you so let's

Tell them to go away
Tell them to go their way
Tell them to accept the love
We nurture in our cove

Standing still

Round and round go the thoughts in my head
Rusty leaves blown away in the autumn air
There is a stillness in the grove
Could it be missing love?

The whispers of the wind in the trees
As far as the eye can see
Not a soul, everything stands still
Feels like even the forest is ill

I cannot hear the birds chirping
I cannot hear the stag bellowing
I cannot hear the fox shrieking
I can only hear my heart crying

I can only hear my heart's longing
Longing for her again, hoping
Hoping to be an "us" again, wishing
Wishing she was in my arms

My arms are where she belongs
I want to feel her breath in mine
I want to feel her lips on mine
I want to feel her heart beat against mine

I want to know I am the one
I want to hold her forever
I want to make her laugh and smile
For her I'd walk a thousand miles

Wolves mate for life

Wolves mate for life
When one leaves, what is life for?
Longing, despair, pain
Where to go, how to escape

The murmurs of the abyss
Tantalizing, seductive
Anything to get out
Anything to stop feeling

Strong and proud is my wolf
But how long until she breaks?
There's a limit somewhere
Anguish, terror, darkness

Feeling cold to the bone
No way to stop it
Freezing, numbing the pain
Could that be it?

Life began when I met her
Attracted by her light
Like moth to a flame
Mesmerized, wanting life

Side by Side
Hand in hand
Heart to Heart
Paw to Paw

My whole wide world

She is my whole wide world
I never realized she could be that bold
I want to make her flash her secret smile
That brings me to my knees mile after mile

For her I would crawl until I am bloody
She is worth every penny
For her I would change all, my ways
She makes me long for yesterdays

I remember us by the ocean
Our first kiss tasting of salt
Her skin so soft, enticing
Her eyes, so mesmerizing

I wish I could turn the wheels of time
But this power is out of reach
I hope she will again be mine
Together lying on a beach

She is my whole wide world
I would do anything for her touches
She is my whole wide world
I love her with all the muches

Hope

I hope to be together again
I hope to ask her hand again
I hope to hold her through the night
Forever more with all my might

I hope we will have another chance
Because we are both out of balance
I know we need each other
To be happy forever

Will she give me another chance
Will she want to come and dance?
Will she realize her mistake
Will she take my hand and partake

In our love once again
Without listening to whispers
Make us both whole again
Holding tight into the wee hours

Staring into each other's eyes
Sharing the same breath
Caressing her soft lips
Just loving her

The wolf's last verses

I feel betrayed like never
Deep to my marrow
I feel so light, it's wonderful
For it did not destroy me,

Feeling so cold when she walked away
So bland is everything
To give up hope, be happy?
Silent goodbye in the forest shroud

She was life's best surprise
The woman who completes me
Love is in the air
She is the one for me

We nurture in our cove
The hope to be whole again
Paw to Paw, they don't know our complicité
We call it crazy love

I love her with all the muches
I wish I still held her close to me
For her I'd walk a thousand miles
I love her forever, for she is my sun

Milton Keynes UK
Ingram Content Group UK Ltd.
UKHW012311160324
439511UK00013B/354